TAMING Party Chaos

TAMING Party Chaos

A Step-by-Step Guide for
Extraordinary Party Planners

By Angel B. L. Elder

Tate Publishing & *Enterprises*

Taming Party Chaos

Cover design by Sommer Buss
Interior design by Lynly Taylor

Published in the United States of America

ISBN: 978-1-5988615-7-0
07.03.12

Dedicated to my husband Robert for his unconditional love and support and to my entire family for their love, laughter, and all the fond memories.

I love you.

TABLE OF CONTENTS

INTRODUCTION

My Grandmother is responsible for this book. She is unquestionably the coolest Grandma in the world. She is one of those people that I can tell anything to simply because she is a wise, generous and phenomenal woman. She has probably seen and heard everything at this point. She *always* has an open front door, cookies in the cookie jar and an ear and a smile for everyone.

She has created a family—a very large family. She and my grandfather have ten children who in turn have lots of children who are now having children of their own. It is great to have four generations of our family around. But, it isn't simply about the size of our family that makes her so wonderful, it is the family dynamic that she created.

She instills the core, the bond, which holds our family together. She teaches us that family is important. That family isn't just being related to someone, it's about being a part of that person's life. That despite the good, the bad and the ugly, the family bond cannot be broken—it may have lots of scar tissue, but it cannot be broken.

My Grandma takes a genuine interest in what's going on with every member of her family and whoever else might be involved at the time with those family members. She really listens.

My theory is that her leadership and her ability to make each of us feel important to her, are the reasons that our family unit is strongly bonded together and is so loving and supportive. The three generations following hers remain so incredibly close because she designed it that way. She taught us that the phrase "being a family" is defined as loving each other, playing together, celebrating all the little things.

She gives us occasions to gather together as a group which helps us to remain an active part of each others' lives. She possesses absolute greatness about her and we honor her.

It is because of her that we each celebrate certain unforgettable family traditions and have millions of fond memories and hilarious stories. It is because of her, that my family, despite its size, gets together for everything and celebrates as a family. Young and old, we celebrate everyone's individual birthdays. We celebrate every religious holiday and some bank holidays. We celebrate all graduations and weddings, and we create special occasions when out-of-towners are in town. Name a reason, event or date; we probably get together and celebrate it.

I love hearing, "we're getting together for breakfast at 9:00am before Aunt and Uncle so-in-so leave town, who all is coming?" When my family goes out to breakfast, we take up half the restaurant.

A crowd can be expected at Grandma's on Halloween either in costume or armed with cameras, and you can bet on her contribution to the kids' candy bags even if it's after bedtime.

I remember as a child, we would go to Grandma's for dinner every Sunday at six o'clock to enjoy one of her dinner specialties, perhaps some of her famous homemade Swedish Meatballs (my favorite).

I really don't know how she isn't sick of cake and ice cream after all the birthday parties over the course of a year or how she never forgets to send a Christmas card and a birthday card.

She has always been there for me and, well, for everybody in our family. Need a ride to sports practice, need a baby sitter, need a place to sleep, need a sounding board, need to tell *somebody* you got engaged, need a place to get your hair & makeup done before a special occasion, need to tell somebody (who will understand) that you just found out you're pregnant, need to feel better after you broke up with your significant other, need a quick stop to use the potty, need to know what happened on your favorite TV Soap Opera, need advice on how to properly pluck your eyebrows or how to shave your face even when you are out of shaving cream? You can count on her. Yes, she even has answers for the boys in the family. Gosh, she knows everything!

I am fortunate to know her, share with her, learn from her and be affected by her. Her name is Agnes Louise Lehr, a.k.a. Aggie, Grandma, Aggie Lou, Mom, Grandma Aggie (never to be called Great Grandma), Mrs. Lehr and Matriarch of the Lehr Clan.

Grandma, I thank you from the bottom of my heart. This is my tribute to you. I love you.

Let me share with you what my Grandma taught me about party planning and hosting, and how to create lots of lasting memories and funny stories of successful, easy-to-do large-group-in-a-small-space-on-a-limited-budget get-togethers.

There are 3 major steps in party planning: Decisions, Designs, and Delivery.

Decisions are to be made well in advance of telling other people about your party. They are the Who's, What's, When's, Why's, Where's and How's of your party, although not necessarily in that order.

Designs are the details of your party and the logistics of it. They are the About's of your party. This is the section when you ask yourself questions such as "How about this?" or "How about that?"

Delivery is the make-it-happen section of your party; the actions, the goings-on, the guts of it. The delivery part is where you find out if everything was worth it. Then there is the moment of truth! The moment of truth is when you, as the host, get verbal and non-verbal feedback from your guests on the success of your party and hosting abilities. No pressure though. With the help of this book, you'll be planning parties with ease and expertise.

Welcome into the mind of a serial party planner—sometimes I just can't help myself . . .

Party planning works for every social gathering whether it is business or pleasure, formal or informal, 2,000+ people or 2 people, adults or children, family or friends, etc. So have no fear, it'll be fun.

Chapter One

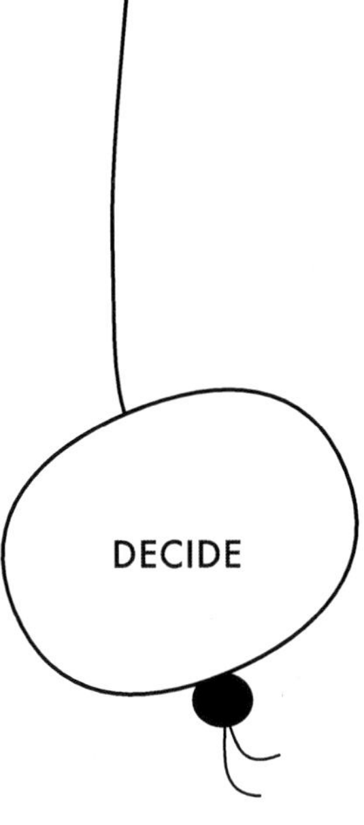

Decide Your Why

First, there are two categories for having a get-together.

Category 1—You have a reason and want to have a party—where the reason came first. For example, your reason may be a Halloween Party or Christmas Party, Religious Holiday or a Birthday Party. There is a pre-existing event that you want to commemorate or celebrate.	Category 2—You want to have a party and need a reason—where the urge for a party came first. For example, any out-of-nowhere get-together such as suddenly deciding to have dinner with friends at home on Sunday at 5:00 P.M., and quickly calling to invite people over for dinner.

Which category is your party in? Why are you having this party? What is the reason? There are plenty of parties in the first category that range all year. Be encouraged to create more in the second category and then incorporate a theme to make it even more fun.

Party Day Suggestions for Category 1:

New Year's Eve	Fourth of July (Independence Day)
Martin Luther King Day	Labor Day
Valentine's Day	Grandparent's Day
Fat Tuesday	Rosh Hashanah
Mardi Gras	Yom Kippur
Ash Wednesday	Boss's Day
St. Patrick's Day	Halloween
Tax Day	Veteran's Day
Tax Refund Day	Thanksgiving Day
Easter	Hanukkah
Secretary's Day	Christmas Eve and Christmas Day
Mother's Day	...and Many More
Memorial Day	
Father's Day	

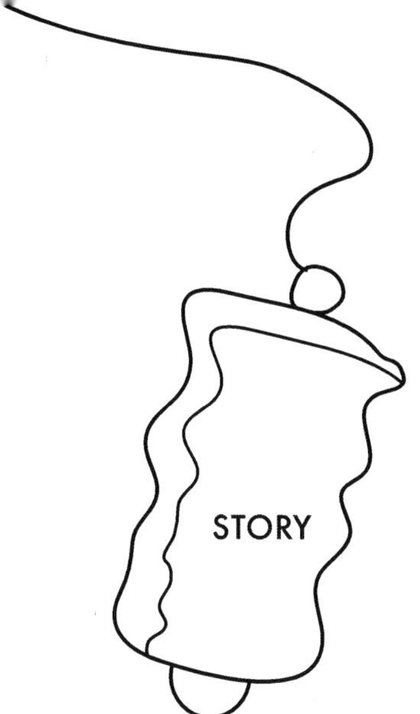

In my family, Thanksgiving is a two-day holiday meaning we get together for the actual holiday and then again the next day to help make a dent in the leftovers. Christmas Eve and Christmas Day become a three-day holiday using the same idea. Memorial Day and Labor Day are BBQ Cookouts with leftovers, but we usually divide up the food and send it home amongst guests in several individual containers. Whatever food remains after the "divide and conquer" ritual, has the "you brought it, you take it" rule applied.

Decide your Themes

You can add a theme to any party regardless of the category. For a party from category 1 where you have a reason and want to have a party, you can have an "Over the Hill" themed birthday party or a "Noah's Ark" baby shower. For a party from category 2 where you want to have a party and need a reason, you can host a "Costume Party" in the middle of March, a "Gag Gift Exchange Party" or a "Ladies Night In Party" where you've hired a masseuse to perform massages on everyone.

Theme Ideas and Basic Suggestions:

Adults Only Parties–no children allowed so you can have party themes based on a more mature guest list.

BBQ Cookout–outdoor party centered around food cooked on the grill and guests bringing or enjoying food on lawn chairs or picnic tables.

Black-Light Party–change out all regular light bulbs with Black Lights so that all white or bright colored fabrics appear to glow.

Bon Fire (permits may be required)–same idea as the BBQ Cookout except at dusk, the host sets up a containment area as a "fire pit" and lights a fire in the middle of the lawn chairs so guests can roast marshmallows, or cook their own hot dogs on an open fire.

Buffet Only / Dinner Out with Large Groups–a no-frills engagement at a buffet restaurant where you simply enjoy the company of your guests.

Candle Light Party–the only light at the party is provided by candles of various sizes.

Canning Food Party (Learn How to)–several people get together to learn how to store food in canning jars, plan this for just after picking all the food out of your garden. Plan to cook/share some of the fresh food with your guests as a thank you for their help.

Children's Parties–endless possibilities based on your child's particular interests, such as race cars or dinosaurs for boys and play dress up or princess parties for girls.

Family Get-Togethers–an informal gathering at someone's house where the guests are mostly family members or very close family friends.

Formal Wear Party–hosted either at home or out a fancy restaurant, where all men are required to wear a tuxedo and all women are required to wear fancy, floor-length gowns.

Gag-Gift Exchange–ask all your guests to each bring one joke gift (used or unwanted) wrapped only in newspaper or in brown paper bags and then put all gifts in a pile. Count the number of guests and write the numbers 1, 2, 3 . . . on small slips of paper and put in a bowl. Have each of your guests draw a number from the bowl and then in order, they will pick a random gift from the pile. Person One will open a gift, person Two can take person One's gift or open a different gift. Person Three can take from person One or Two or choose a different gift to unwrap and so on until every guest has opened one. Note: as host of this party, plan to have a few extra gag gifts wrapped and ready to go so that everyone can participate, even those who may have forgotten to bring a gift.

Going Away to Jail Party–this is either to say goodbye to someone who is actually going to jail or as a joke theme party where all guests show up in costume as inmates wearing black & white striped garments or bright orange jumpsuits with their inmate number on the front and back of the jump suit.

DECIDE

Graduation Party–similar to a Birthday party except the cake has a sugar-paper picture of the graduate instead of candles.

Hawaiian Luau–all guests come dressed in Hawaiian dresses and shirts, usually with bright colors and large flowers on them. Play Hawaiian music on the stereo by purchasing a CD. In addition, the host can make or purchase a theme-based volcano cake to serve to your guests. Also, your guests can learn some traditional Hawaiian dances to add to the party atmosphere and fun.

Kiss-the-Cook Party–the cook, or guest of honor, wears an apron that says "kiss the cook" and anyone who talks to or gets caught looking at the guest of honor has to "kiss the cook" on the cheek. The cook, or guest of honor, is required to obnoxiously draw attention to himself/herself throughout the entire event and all other guests are required to make sure anyone owing a kiss to guest of honor pays up immediately.

Laser Tag Party–hosted at an official Laser Tag Center, all guests schedule a time to be in the laser tag room and then try to shoot at each other with lasers and try to avoid being shot. The center will keep score for you and let you know who the sharp-shooter is. This is a fun activity that keeps guests moving as they run around, however for those who can't run, go ahead and suggest they still participate by finding a "sniper" spot where they can shoot others without being found out. It is best to schedule the first round for the group, and then stay out one session to relax and talk to your guests, then go back in for another round of play. Sessions range in time and price, call first to get information from your local laser tag center.

New Business Kick Off Party–invite friends and business associates and surrounding businesses to this party to spread the word and show off your new business. Order simple foods to share like pizza and soda pop or have it catered. Have fliers and business cards on hand for your guests to take with them. Be sure to give tours of your building to anyone who attends. Remember to invite your bankers, accountants, doctors; anyone who may help you spread the word about your new business.

Out-of-Towners are In-Town Today Party–either go out to eat in the honor of your out-of-town guests or plan to eat in, but tell all your guests that the gathering is for your out-of-town people.

Pool Party–best hosted at a private residence so you have the pool for your guests only and not the general public. Tell them to bring or wear swimsuits and to bring a towel. You can supply the food, cook on the grill or ask guests to bring a dish to share.

Potluck Dinner—this is the easiest to pull off. Ask each of your guests to bring a dish to share. As the host, plan for your contribution to be a main course dish and beverages since most of your guests will likely bring a side dish or dessert. If you choose, you can always request that your guests bring their own beverages.

Road Rally Scavenger Hunt–this is a complex game for large groups where you as the host have laid out clues for cars of two or four people to find then follow. Each clue will lead them to the next clue, then the next clue and so on until they reach the end where you are waiting for them with a prize of free food or a First Place ribbon.

Snow Birds Pool Party–same as a Pool Party, see above description, except have this party in December or January, when it is most cold in your area. Unless you have totally outrageous, fun-loving, crazy friends, it is recommended that it be a heated outdoor pool or an indoor pool.

Name	Phone	Address	Email	Total No.	Expect No.	Xmas Card	Gift	Invite Sent
Elder, Angel & Husband								
Friend, Mr.								
Family, Aunt Mary								
TOTALS								

Decide your Who (Guest List)

Now that you know why you are having a party and if you are having a theme for it, you need to decide who will be invited.

The first step in creating your guest list is to make a master list. Put the names of *everyone you know* on this master list and include all pertinent information on it. Include personal friends, neighbors, business associates, and your friends' friends.

I suggest using a spreadsheet on a computer or contact management software so you can easily modify and update your list. It also helps when you need to count the total number of people invited or when you need to print it out.

The spreadsheet headings I use are: Last Name, First Name (including Spouse/Significant Other), Children's Names, Phone Number, E-mail (if you will ever send invitations this way), Total Number (in household), Expect Number (how many I expect to actually show up, since some people never come despite your invitation), Invitation Sent (Use a check mark or an "X" for YES and leave blank for NO), and Number to Attend (based on actual RSVP's). I use the auto-sum icon to have the computer supply me with a running total at the bottom of my spreadsheet so that I can look at my numbers and see instantly how many people I've invited, and how many are actually coming. During the holiday season, I add "Christmas Card Sent" and "Gift" headings for people I mail items to.

This spreadsheet system has been invaluable to me and works remarkably for every party. When I meet new people, I simply add them to the master list so I don't forget them when I am preparing for my next party.

Feel free to alter your list to fit your needs. If you want to add a heading for important dates like "Birthday" or "Anniversary" go ahead.

Once you have your master list created you can select only the people you want for any particular party. If you are getting married, you'll probably invite everyone, but if you are just having dinner, you can simply eliminate people who likely will be unable to attend, such as those who live out of state. If you are hosting an adult's only party you can eliminate the children and those who may be offended by your theme—you know who they are!

I first developed and used the spreadsheet idea when I was engaged for the first time and was planning the guest list for the wedding. I created the list so I would have all the names and addresses in one spot. This would not only speed up the process of getting our invitations mailed out but we could also easily track who we invited, who had responded and how many mouths we were going to feed that night. It turns out, we had a lot more friends than we thought and I had a LOT MORE family than he thought. We had a catering budget for about 200 people. Exceeding that number was easy even before we added his family!

I kept that original spreadsheet concept, which is appropriately named "Guest List", and when we called off the wedding and our engagement, I simply deleted his friends and family from my list.

Having found the love of my life since then, my current spreadsheet has a complete list of my husband, Robert's, family and grows constantly as I add new friends and new family members. The point is the spreadsheet idea is an easy and awesome tool for guest lists.

Decide your When (Date and Time)

The next step in party planning is to decide the date and time of your gathering. Both date AND time need to be considered together.

Answer these questions:

- How long do you need in order to pull off the occasion you've planned? Do you need one hour or eight hours, or somewhere in between?
- How many of your guests will stay the entire time?
- What day has that amount of time open?

Business parties should be scheduled during the business week and as close to the work day as possible. Ideally, work parties would be during the work day, not after. Social/Personal parties need to avoid the working hours of the business day. Ideally, social parties would be held on the weekend when most people are available. There are always exceptions, of course. One example of an exception is hosting a dinner party that would begin after normal business hours and would end in time for your guests to be home at a decent hour. During the week, free time is more precious and the host needs to be conscious of that.

Don't schedule a party at a poor time. A poor time is defined as a time at which very few people will be able to attend. Do make your party at a convenient time for as many guests as possible. For example, you probably don't want to have your child's birthday party at your house during the week at 2:00 P.M. because most parents are working and can't make it. However, if your guest list consists mostly of kids from school and you can have the party at your child's school; it will be more likely to go over well at 2:00 P.M. on a weekday.

Be careful with Start and End times, especially End times. Only use End times if you must be done by a certain time. If you have rented a banquet hall, for example, you may have a certain time frame within to use the hall and therefore End times would be important. Some halls charge hefty late fees if you are not out of the building by the designated End time. However, if you are at home and have all day/night to let your party go on, then leave the End time off your invitation; otherwise some guests may leave a lively party early because they believed that you were going to enforce the End you stated on your invitation.

Whatever your start time, make sure you have enough time for your party to feel relaxed and fun, while avoiding having it drag on all day with nothing for your guests to do. See the Activities section of this book for ideas.

Decide your Where (Location)

Where are you having your party? Picking a location is easy. The most common location choice is your home, either indoor or outdoor or both. The majority of this book assumes an at home party, whether it's your house or a friend's house, although these planning ideas can be used elsewhere. Other location choices are banquet halls, restaurants, other people's houses, parks, community centers, club houses, the beach, conference/convention centers and many others.

Answer these questions:

- Which place suits your needs and will fit the number guests you've invited?
- Does your location have restroom facilities for your guests?
- Does your location allow for inclement weather?
- What can you afford?

Many people feel that their homes are not large enough or nice enough for a party. The truth is that if there is room for more than one person, there is room for party, even if it is a small one. Parties don't have to be fancy and the place settings on the table don't have to match. Even having 2–3 friends over can turn into a great party. Don't be limited by old beliefs that are standing in your way of a great time.

Decide your How (Solo Host or Co-Host)

If you are planning a small, simple party, you can likely host it yourself. If you are creating a larger, more complicated type (wedding or such) you may want some help. If this is your first time, and are nervous about hosting a party, or just want to share the responsibility, then co-host a party with someone else. The key is to pick a trustworthy co-host.

If co-hosting, pick a good friend who will be there early to help you prepare AND who will stay late to help you clean up. If they can't do both, then pass. Also, discuss your ideas and plans beforehand. You definitely do not want to have differences of opinion while your party is going on.

Whether you solo host or co-host your party, make sure you enjoy yourself. Most guests look to the host(s) to set the tone of a party before they relax into it. Your guests will sense if you are in a poor mood, or if you are upset about something, and it will take its toll on your party. If, on the other hand, you are having the time of your life, are relaxed, cool, calm and collected, then your party will reflect that too!

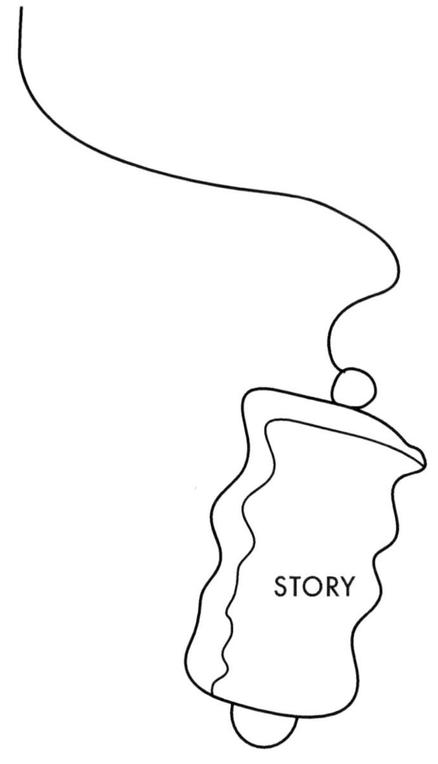

I co-hosted a party at a friend's house. The party was originally my idea, and he agreed to have it at his house. About 30 of the guests invited showed up for it. He was very, very nervous about it, but did a fantastic job preparing for this party. He did more than I could ever have asked him to do. He painted the interior of his house, had his pool cleaned and prepared after years of disuse, had trees removed from the backyard and bought all the food. He even bought new chairs and a new rolling dry bar to serve drinks on for the party. I was incredibly impressed!

Yet, he was very nervous about the party. I was concerned because he was so nervous he might, at the last minute, not show up that I had him give me a key to his house. My thought was, "I wasn't going to host a party that I couldn't get into".

I, being the co-host, arrived early. He wasn't home. So I called him on his cell phone, fearing the worst. He said he was picking up the party trays of food and would be back shortly. I was relieved to hear it. So, I started doing some minor rearranging of the furniture to allow for better traffic flow, and started visualizing aspects of the party (we'll talk about that in a later chapter). When he returned, I helped him unload all the food and set it out on the tables. When guests began to arrive, he began to get a bit uptight, became more stressed and wasn't dressed for the party yet. I told him that, "yes, some people do arrive exactly on time" and encouraged him to go get ready.

Everything was going smoothly until the sun began to set outside and I went around his house turning on lights. I felt it was getting too dark. He kept going behind me and turning them off and getting really upset with me. Finally, I took him outside, where no one would hear us and asked him what the problem was. Apparently, he didn't want all the lights on as he thought it would ruin the soft mood of the party, while I was thinking this is a party in a house, not in a cave and that we needed to brighten it up to keep the mood pleasant. I told him, if he has a problem with something, to talk it out to me right here, right now—not around the guests. After venting a few words of frustration, we agreed that everyone else was having a good time and we agreed that we would turn on only the dim lights. We compromised.

The rest of the party went very well; everyone enjoyed themselves and the party ended sometime after 2:30A.M. I learned, when I co-host, to discuss all the party details ahead of time so there isn't a difference of opinion during the party.

DECIDE

Decide your What (Food and Drink Options)

Decide first who is supplying the food and beverages. Are you, the host, offering everything or is it going to be a bring-a-dish-to-share (a.k.a. Potluck style)? Not sure? Consider how much you want, or have, to spend on food and how much time you have to prepare it all.

If you are on a limited budget, go for potluck style. If you have plenty of money to spend, then go ahead and splurge a bit on your guests and have it catered. They will appreciate it. If you don't have a lot of time, choose potluck style or simply pre-order food trays from your local grocery store. Party trays are already prepared and ready for you to pick up on the day of your party.

When hosting a potluck style party and a guest asks you what you want them to bring, suggest a specific type of food or drink. Don't say, "Whatever you want, you decide". It is better to tell them something! Say, "Bring pasta salad, or bring a bottle of pop, or bring chips . . ." Give them one or two simple, easy-to-buy, easy-to-bring, or easy-to-make ideas. You will want to let them know that it is okay with you that they have bought something from the store and that they don't have to personally make/prepare the dish they bring.

People will sometimes avoid coming to your party because, to them, it is too much pressure deciding what to bring. Believe me, I've had it happen.

I'd much rather have my guests at the party with a bottle of Coca-Cola or store-bought cupcakes than not show up at all. Besides, if you tell people different things to bring, you will avoid having almost everyone bring the same thing—a dessert. I made that error once.

I hosted a very informal Potluck style dinner and invitations were done by phone. I didn't specify what I wanted people to bring, and didn't request RSVP's so I had no idea who was coming or what food they were bringing. I had designed it to be that way. It was supposed to be a comfortable dinner party with whoever showed up, with emphasis on dinner. I made large quantities of homemade lemonade, mashed potatoes, and my grandmother's famous date-nut pudding. I figured with the possible options of main dish, side dish, drinks, and dessert that I'd covered most of them with my offerings—everything but a main dish. I thought I was in good shape.

My guests started arriving. Some people brought side dishes like fresh vegetables trays from the store and pasta salads, and others brought home-made spinach salad and fruit salad; and other guests brought beverages. But the interesting thing was more and more people arrived with dessert . . . dessert after dessert after dessert. We had many kinds of cookies, several pies, a couple of large cakes, strudels, cheesecake, and plenty of date-nut pudding, etc. but NO MAIN COURSE! We all ate until we were full and about 10 pounds heavier! As the host, I didn't freak out and get all upset. Actually, I remained in my great state of mind, still had a good time and enjoyed all the leftover desserts! My guests and I all joked about it being a dessert party, not a dinner party. I learned to take a different approach to potluck the next time.

If you are supplying all the food for the party, make sure you have a variety of foods available. Keep in mind that you may have invited the "give it to me, I'll eat anything" types of people along with the health-conscious "strictly vegan" vegetarian types to your party as well. So a variety will be much appreciated. Don't worry; no one will force you to eat the leftover vegetables before you can eat dessert.

Here are two hints that all meat-eating hosts need to know about vegetarians:

1. Salad is not the only non-meat meal option and
2. It is okay to ask a vegetarian what they will eat at a party; it is not a taboo subject.

Your vegetarian guests will likely be grateful that you are aware of their eating habits and are taking them into consideration. What an incredible host you are to think of EVERYTHING . . .

It's a good idea to have beverages available throughout entire party while serving the snack foods, main foods and desserts at different times. Serve beverages and snack foods immediately, as soon as guests begin to arrive. Snack foods include: chips & dip, pretzels, cheese & crackers, fresh fruits and vegetables cut into finger foods, nacho chips and salsa, etc.

> HINT: breads tend to swell when mixed with liquids and will fill people up. Full people are happy people, and happy people can take their time when eating the more costly main course foods.

After a good amount of the snack foods have been nibbled on, serve the main foods. The main foods include: sandwiches, salads, pasta, meats, and anything cooked like grilled salmon/chicken/shrimp/hot dogs/hamburgers/ribs/veggies, various kinds of -kabobs, steak, corn on the cob, soups, etc. Then, very shortly after or even immediately after serving the main foods, open and serve the dessert. Since you don't want lots of food left over, put everything out for your guests that you want eaten. You may want to make a list of foods you want to serve at your party so that food dishes will not be forgotten. I once made a pasta salad before a party started and put it in the refrigerator so it would stay cold. Ironically, I forgot to set it out when my guests arrived, and discovered it later when I was putting away the left-overs after the party was over.

Here's a hint: some desserts may be considered "too pretty to eat", so go ahead and cut into cakes and pies so that your guests will actually eat them. This seems only to come up for desserts; people have no qualms about digging into the perfect green bean casserole or the perfect bean dip or the perfect cheese ball. No one knows why!

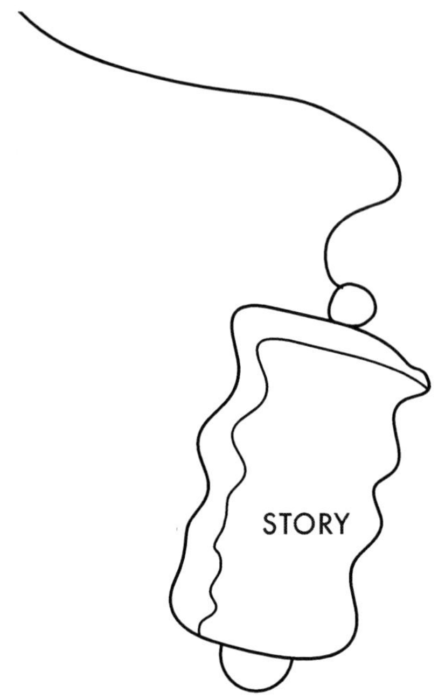

Speaking of desserts that are too pretty to eat, I had the perfect cake at my "College Graduation Party". This cake was made by the neighborhood grocery store bakery department. My cake had an edible sugar-paper picture of me in my graduation cap and gown. It was a beautiful cake and a great picture of me, if I do say so myself. Since my sisters must have thought it was just too pretty to eat, they promptly carved a mustache and beard into my photo on the cake—and thought it was just hilarious! They made a point of bringing my attention to it before passing the blame onto each other and never admitting guilt. I guess some things will never change from childhood. Even to this day, I still don't know who actually did the defacing.

Decide your What (Wardrobe)

What are you going to wear? This issue isn't as big as it used to be. Dress appropriately, not over- or under-dressed. For a casual party, you can wear jeans and a t-shirt or dress pants and a nicer shirt/blouse. For a very casual, wear shorts and a t-shirt. When deciding what to wear, keep in mind that wearing the color white to a barbeque is not recommended, since Murphy's Law says you'll wear the BBQ sauce home. The point here is to be comfortable, and to dress for various temperatures. Have a change of clothes handy if there is a chance you may be too hot or too cold.

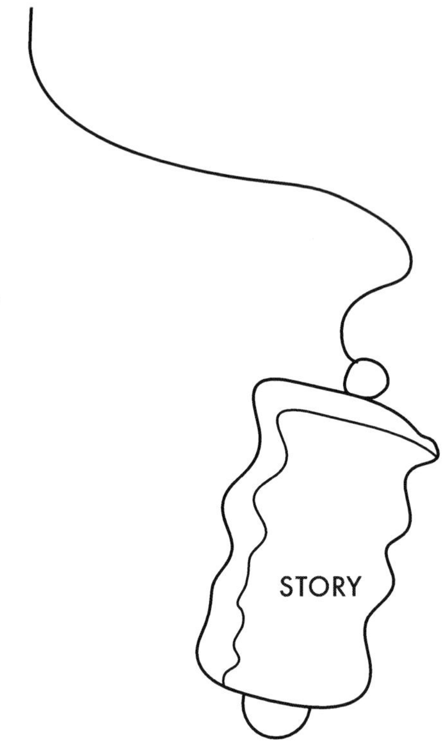

My family gets together for the 4th of July every year. Since July is one of the few warm months in Michigan, most people wear shorts and t-shirts. It is very casual.

Our tradition is to congregate in the driveway between my grandmother's house and my Aunt Mary's house (which is now owned by my cousin). We gather for a BBQ around 6 P.M. or so, and everyone shows up. It is potluck style, and everyone brings their specialty dishes. Aunt Anne brings her famous pasta/spaghetti salad. Aunt Joan brings her famous cookies (home made, of course). My Uncle Ron fires up the grill and monitors the hamburgers, hot dogs, sausage, ribs, steaks, and corn on the cob—which are then cooked to perfection. There is a selection of fresh finger-foods like grapes, baby carrots, celery, and cauliflower served with veggie dip. Then, there has to be a watermelon which is a favorite of my cousin Joey's.

We eat and gossip, and eat some more. As the sun begins to set, we spray ourselves down with bug spray and change into long-sleeved shirts or jackets and into jeans to keep from looking like we suffer from chicken pox after all the mosquito bites.

Then we pack up the food (temporarily), load into the closest vehicles like sardines, and drive or walk to our family's "secret" parking spot.

Next, we grab various blankets, strollers, lawn chairs and whatever children need to be accounted for and we walk to our self-designated family spot to watch the fireworks over the river. Miraculously, no one takes our spot. Perhaps it's because we have done this for so many years; perhaps it's the sheer size of our group that keeps others away. I guess we'll never know.

After the grand finale of the fireworks, we again grab our various blankets, strollers, lawn chairs and children and we return to the cars, trucks and vans and head back. Within minutes, all the food is back out on the buffet table and the grill is hot and ready for the next round. We eat again, and gossip some more. After a while, people begin to leave and when we're all stuffed again to the bursting point, we encircle the portable fire pit and those of us remaining discuss life's most challenging and introspective topics like, "Why is it, that there is ALWAYS some idiot who drives through the crowd of people with bright headlights on after the fireworks have started—knowing full well that all the street lights are off and there are thousands of people, children included, sitting in the dark, in the road, watching the fireworks?" We may never figure this one out.

By the end, we have two sets of dirty clothes: a t-shirt and a pair of shorts and a long-sleeved shirt or jacket along with a pair of jeans that smell of bug spray and smoke from the fire pit. Dirtying up two sets of clothes is worth it though, since a good time is had by all.

DECIDE

If it's a theme party, the same applies. Dress appropriately and participate. If it's a Halloween party, wear a costume. If it's a toga party, show up in sheets. If it's a worst-dressed contest, show up in a fire-engine red shirt with yellow and orange flowers and bright lime-green polyester pants that are a size too small! If it's a Hawaiian Luau, wear the same fire-engine red shirt with yellow and orange flowers and . . . wait, skip the polyester pants, better to go with a bathing suit underneath. If the party is formal, ladies, wear a floor-length gown. You deserve it! Guys, wear a tuxedo. Rent one, or better yet, buy one. It a known fact that every man looks awesome and very sexy in a tuxedo; there is no way around it. Your date will thank you.

The point is to participate. If you host a theme party, you will need to be dressed to set a standard for the party. How can you expect guests to play at 100%, if the host won't?

Decide your What (Activities, Contests & Games)

What are your guests going to DO? Yes, you *can* have a party with no activities planned. However, they tend to be shorter, the guests leave earlier, and there are more eerie silences and weird moments. If most of your guests already know each other, a no-plans party is easier to pull off. But if you have invited a lot of different people who don't already know each other, you will need something to get them talking and keep them interested.

Activities should begin with a simple tour of your location, followed by you, the host, introducing strangers to each other and mentioning if they have a shared interest, background, challenge, problem or idea.

Contests and games are great for creating participation, conversation, friendly competition, team building, fond memories, and sometimes a blackmail photo or two. In either event, good times are had. The point is to get (and keep) your guests involved. If they are involved, the will feel welcome, accepted, and they will think you are a great host when they have an enjoyable time.

Game Ideas

Cards	Interactive/team games:
Dominoes	Pictionary
Board games	Gestures
Voting for best/worst ____ (fill in the blank)	Charades
	Ping Pong
Bridal/Baby Bingo	Twister

If you need game ideas, head to your nearest Wal-Mart and walk down the game aisle and pick a game or make up a game of your own.

Pay attention to your guests. If you notice that people seem bored, then take action to change it. Start an activity or change the music, serve food early, ask for people to help you do something. This will re-energize the people and "stir the pot" so to speak. The same goes if it feels too rushed, be flexible enough to slow down. In order to slow down, you may have to eliminate one or two of your planned activities. Keep in mind, regardless of how awesome your activities are, you can save them for your next party.

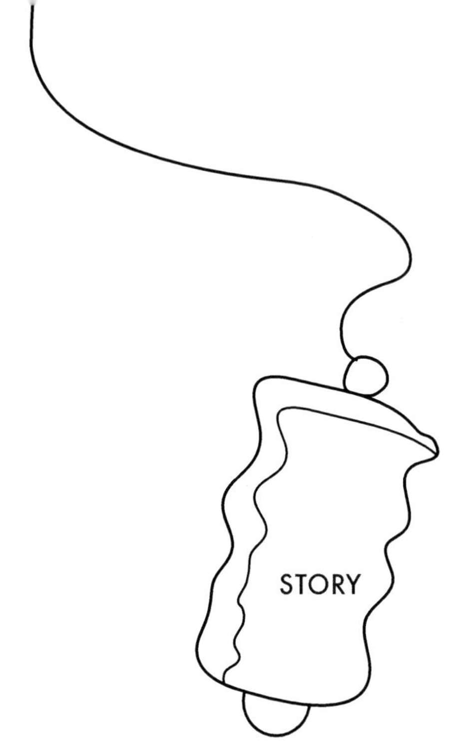

I hosted a New Year's Eve party. In years past, a select group of close friends of mine get together on New Year's Eve and we celebrated our accomplishments over the past year while sharing great food and then we set goals for the upcoming year. These people have become my family away from my real family and this annual party has become somewhat of a family tradition for me. The only challenge we found was with such great people and the fantastic stories they tell about their accomplishments, we were going later and later into the night with our goal setting. So this year, we tried something new.

We had the first annual two-part New Year's party. The first part, I dubbed "the celebration" and the second part, I named "the commitment". On New Year's Eve, we had just the party part with food and beverages and games and on the following day, we reconvened to commit to new goals using a more stringent timing, more like a business meeting with a start time and an end time.

Because we had all agreed to open up our smaller group to invite anyone else who wanted to come, I had planned for several more people than actually showed up to the New Year's Eve party. In anticipation of newcomers, I had created a couple of new games to help people to get to know each other better. I entitled one game, "Whose Achievement is it Anyway?" Another game had a series of questions to open up discussion such as "Before tonight, you may not have known this about me ___________. Who am I?" The idea was to get people talking and to gently celebrate accomplishments without being hard nosed about it.

As it turned out, the people who showed up to the party were already part of this close group of friends so we all knew each other. Coincidentally, we to started playing a game called "Cash Flow 101" and we were so engrossed in the excitement of the game that we almost missed the countdown to midnight. Keep in mind, the Cash Flow 101 game was not one of the activities I had planned on. But since I didn't insist on playing the games I *had* planned on playing, the party went even better than expected. Sometimes the host should just go with the flow and energy of the party and not be a stickler for the original itinerary.

DECIDE

your Why–reason and theme

your Who–guest list

your When–date & time

your Where–location

your How–host solo or with help

your What–food, wardrobe & activities

Chapter Two

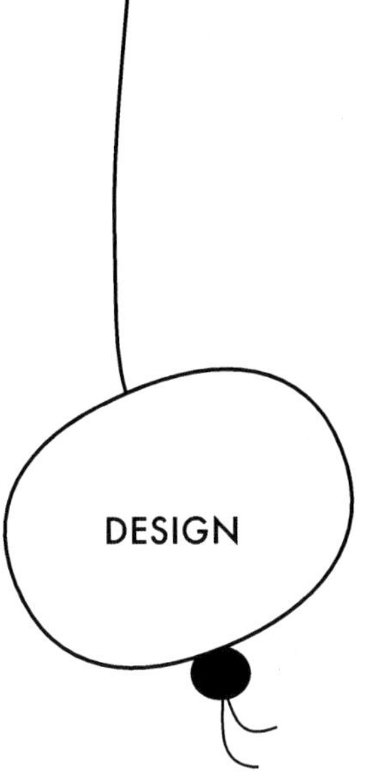

The Design stage is the creative step and the most fun (next to the actual party, of course). This is where you get to make your masterpiece and put all the details together. I said earlier that this is where the logistics of your party are developed and executed.

Design your Atmosphere / Mood

What is the mood of your party going to be?

Uplifting and fun?	Scheduled and apportioned?
Soft and sensual?	Gender specific?
Personal and close?	Business oriented?
Open and friendly?	Casual?

Your atmosphere will help determine the mood of your party along with other aspects like the appropriate invitations, decorations, and layout.

Design your Invitations

You will design your invitations based on the aspects you have determined so far. Your invitations should relate directly to your party and invoke a positive reaction of some kind. They should also be distributed in a manner that is appropriate.

Invitations will include all of the following important information:

Purpose (is usually on front of invitation)	Directions
Date	What to bring
Time(s)	What to wear or how to dress
Location (use exact address, do not write only "my house")	Any other important details your guests may need to know beforehand

Your invitations can reflect a theme or a mood. For example, if you are hosting a baby shower with a Noah's Ark theme, the invitation could have cartoon animals on it, or be related to bible stories. If you are hosting a Halloween party, your invitations could have pumpkins or ghosts or the words "Trick-or-Treat" on them.

Where do you shop for invitations or specialty paper? There are lots of options. Most grocery stores have theme invitations for common holidays like Christmas and Halloween and are very easy to find. These small packages, usually of 10 or 20, work well if you are having a small party. Although, they can be a bit costly and you will have to hand-write all your party details on each one individually.

For larger gatherings, office supply stores will sell card stock (heavier, thicker) paper, perforated cards and various printed stationery if you want to print your own at home on your personal computer/printer. Those of you who, like me, don't have the best penmanship should use a printer or have someone else hand-write your invitations. I use my printer for everything. Making your own invitations is cheaper than ordering invitations.

Stationery paper comes in different colors, with all kinds of pictures or borders, and may even be packaged with matching envelopes.

Print shops like Kinko's also sell stationery paper. They can offer printing and design services for you. Using a print shop with an experienced staff is a good idea if you need a certain professional look or raised print. Check your local print shops/copy shops for their prices before deciding to venture this way.

For business invitations, if your party is less formal (invitees are close associates within your department or your team), then it is okay to send an invitation by e-mail. If your business party is more formal and your company image is important, like for inviting existing and potential customers, prestigious executives or important community leaders, have your invitations specially printed on thick, perhaps embossed or high-gloss paper with your company name and/or logo on it. Don't go cheap. It is very important that your formal business invitations make the very best impression.

Invitations can be distributed by using the telephone, sending e-mail (when appropriate as noted above), handing out fliers, and by mailing cards or formal invitations. A formal invitation usually means there is extra care to produce them and often times there are multiple pieces to your invitation. The most common example of a formal invitation is a wedding invitation.

Use the telephone when you are inviting your immediate family and close friends, when your party is very informal, or when you have missed the mailing deadline (the invitations would probably arrive by mail after the party date or with too little notice). Use e-mail for informal business invitations or for close friends who you are absolutely certain WILL check their e-mail and get your invitation. I don't recommend e-mailing as a way to get the word out. There are too many problems, technical difficulties and time constraints to rely on e-mail. How many times have you heard the following:

> "I got so much junk mail that I changed my e-mail address . . ."
>
> "My system/network/computer is down . . ."
>
> "My computer has a virus and all my stuff is gone . . ."
>
> "There is something wrong with my e-mail . . ."
>
> "Sorry, I just didn't have time to check my e-mail . . ."
>
> Not to mention, e-mail can be deemed impersonal.

Use fliers if everybody in the universe is invited to your party, as these are easy to duplicate, hand out, and leave a stack in public places. Fliers also provide lots of information in the space provided and can be mailed without an envelope when taped closed. Using printed multicolor stationery paper is nicer than using a ream of one-color paper. Most fliers are printed on one-color paper. If you use stationery paper you should then fold them neatly in thirds, and mail them in envelopes. Folded cards and formal invitations will require envelopes.

Be sure to include directions to your location with your invitation. You may even want to include a road map showing your location. You can describe step-by-step driving directions or you can simply have a small physical map of the major roads nearby that lead to your event spot.

One more thought about invitations, if each invitation is especially thick, heavy, or if it has multiple pieces to it, have it weighed at the post office or with a postage scale. Make sure you have the correct amount of postage on each invitation. You don't want your invitations returned to you—undelivered, simply because there wasn't enough postage.

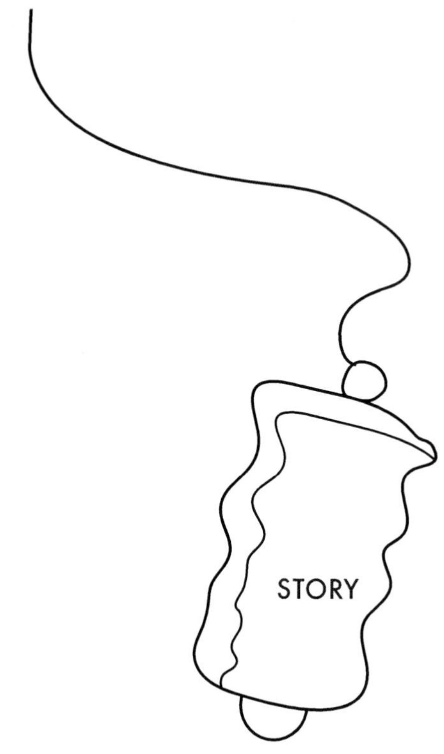

My best friend Cindy mailed out her beautiful wedding invitations about three months before her wedding. Her wedding reception was to be held in an antique ballroom in a historic part of downtown Detroit, MI. The only problem was that there was limited seating. So she had to limit her guest list to her very closest family and friends. She mailed out invitations to her immediate family and honored guests (myself included) and had planned that with every declined invitation she could then invite another guest, in plenty of time, to fill the seats and get as many friends in attendance as possible.

I received a phone call from her asking me if I had received her invitation. I responded that yes I had, but why was she asking. She stated that some of her invitations had been returned for insufficient postage. Apparently, some had been delivered, some had been returned, and who knows what happened to the rest.

This is an issue that every bride-to-be can do without. Unfortunately, it happened to my dear friend.

(Side note: I have to give her credit for creativity, having two rounds of invitations was a great idea I hadn't heard of at the time.) Despite the challenging experience she endured, as with any great host, she didn't let the road blocks get in the way of her enjoyment of the planning process and she pulled off a fantastic wedding ceremony and reception. I'd like to add that the day she got married, is the same day that my husband proposed to me. Sharing that day with Robert *and* my best friend on her perfect day was an incredible party experience.

Design your Decorations

Your decorations will help you to set a mood and create an atmosphere. Keep in mind having too many decorations can look tacky or busy and having too few decorations can go unnoticed which will ultimately be a waste of your time and money.

Most parties don't need decorations. However, when you decide you want decorations, you can have a lot of fun with them.

There is a wide range of decorations you can choose from, everything from making them by hand to purchasing them. If you want to make decorations, you can use construction paper and cut it into strips, staple the ends together to create a loop and, by connecting the loops together, make a chain out of different colored loops. This is popular with children and teachers and it is a fantastic family activity. Purchasing and displaying decorations can be as simple as balloons and crepe paper streamers taped to the ceiling, or as elaborate as hiring a decorator to decorate a hall for a wedding with colorful, coordinating balloon arches and back-lit ice sculptures.

Candles are a great way to use decorations to create a mood. They are often inexpensive and are an easy decoration to add on to. Not only do they change the lighting, they add color and can add fragrance (I recommend strongly-scented candles.) Candles can be plain with a glass jar or be placed on a mirror along with some fresh-cut ivy leaves for a more classic look.

Store-bought decorations for famous occasions like Christmas or Halloween are very easy. You buy them and hang them up or place them on a table. They are common and can be found just about everywhere. It makes them very convenient. The only downside is they can get expensive when you want to have a large number of decorations or if you have a large area to decorate.

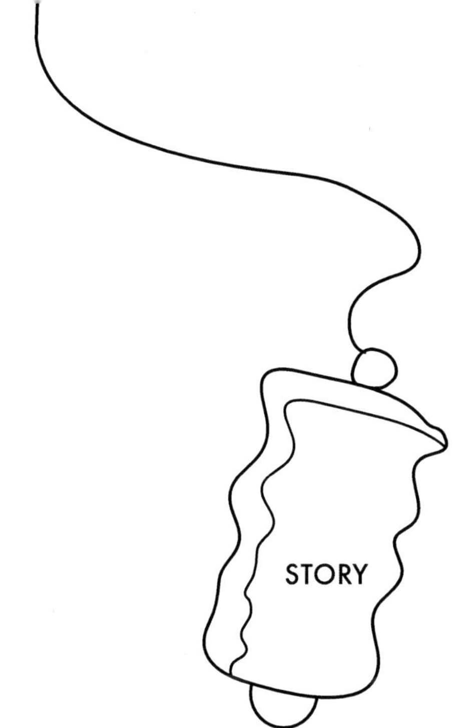

When my Aunt Joan got engaged, they announced their engagement in the local newspaper. They figured it was the only way to reach their entire respective families–and it was! It was also a lot cheaper than trying to call everyone. My Aunt is the 6th child out of 10 in her generation and her hubby-to-be is the 11th child out of 12 in his generation of his family. Talk about a BIG wedding!

My Aunt held her wedding reception at the Community Center in Gibraltar, MI. This community center isn't the most spectacular place, but it has large, open rooms with kitchen facilities and the added bonus of more than one stall in the Lady's Restroom. The biggest thing this place has going for it, is that it is large enough to accommodate my whole family at an affordable price! My aunt and newest uncle went with a 4th of July theme as their wedding was the end of June. They had made many of their own decorations. As guests walked to the door of the community center, they saw paper rockets lining

DESIGN

the walkway. The rockets were made from paper towel rolls and cut paper. The paper rockets were stuck on sticks standing up out of the grass along the sidewalk. Inside, the bride and groom had homemade construction paper fireworks hanging from the ceiling by strings that allowed the "fireworks" to move; they had sparkly table decorations along with noise makers and pull-string poppers that throw confetti everywhere and the used balloons to showcase their table where they sat to eat dinner. Right after the first dance, balloons fell from the ceiling for the "balloon drop".

In keeping with the theme, at the designated time after the sunset, everyone was handed sparklers and we walked outside. The sparklers, specifically called "morning glories," are safer, more colorful than normal sparklers and are recommended for use with large crowds and for use by children. Each sparkler had a matchbook tied to it with the bride and groom's name on it as a keepsake that was also useful. This made it easier for the guests to light their own sparkler.

My Aunt and Uncle had arranged for an impressive, full-scale fireworks display for all of the guests in attendance. It began with a picturesque moment with the bride and groom standing in front of cascade of sparklers called a "waterfall". It looked like a brilliantly colored curtain behind them all glowing in white light against the dark night background. Their wedding photographer had a special camera to capture them on film with these real fireworks in the background at night. (They searched specifically for someone with this expertise and with great talent for night/dark pictures. After all, these were their wedding photos.) Next, the huge full-scale fireworks display began and lasted several minutes. To give some idea, this fireworks show would easily rival the size of the show put on by small cities like Gibraltar on the Fourth of July.

My aunt said that even she and her new husband were awestruck by the beauty of the fireworks and that her photos turned out so perfect that the photos were in the newspaper to announce their wedding to everyone. Perhaps the local newspaper should be renamed the Lehr Family Tribune. To top the night off, everyone finally lit their respective sparklers in honor of the bride and groom.

Please note: They had legally prearranged to have the appropriate city-required permits, had the Gibraltar Fire Department on site the entire time and had hired professional pyrotechnicians to run the fireworks show. Fireworks are very dangerous and many are illegal for private use. Do not attempt any kind of fireworks show or use of fire of any kind without proper preparation and safety measures in place.

By the way, having the Fire Department wasn't a bad idea since there was a slight timing issue that had the bride and groom running for cover. Apparently, even with careful planning and timing, the in-the-sky fireworks show started a couple of minutes too soon and before anyone could do anything about it, fragments of rocket shells began falling on the bride and groom. Some fragments were still on fire! My Aunt, my uncle, and their photographer ran for safety under the nearest park pavilion outside the community center. Fortunately, no one was hurt, and my aunt now has a great wedding story to pass on to her future grandchildren.

The wedding and the fireworks presentation were breathtaking (and not just from running for safety). Sorry, had to throw that in.

This is a fantastic example of to turn the "blah and empty" into the "beautiful and exciting"!

Design your Spatial Layout / Floor Plan

When designing your spatial layout and floor plan use the water principle. The *water principle* is that water travels on the path of least resistance. Pretend that your guests are the water. Put furniture in a way that there is easy traffic flow for your party.

DESIGN

You may be used to walking around complicated floor plans and dodging the sharp corners of your glass coffee table, but your guests aren't. Allow them to walk and travel in straight lines or on soft curves around your furniture and tables, through rooms and in buffet lines.

Good rule of thumb: No 90 degree angles allowed.

Also, create wide open spaces to walk through. A good test is: if you have to turn sideways or on an angle in order to get around furniture, or to get through a door, then make some changes to the floor plan.

Some Suggestions:

Move your couch out of the way or put a chair in the corner to soften the angle.

If you expect people to walk completely around a table, put it in the middle of your room, with lots of space on all sides at least 36 inches.

If you don't expect people to walk all the way around a table, then put it as close to a wall as possible.

Open doors as far as they will go, move small items like trash cans out of the way.

Put chairs against the walls facing the center of the room or slightly facing other chairs.

Make sure any electrical cords are safely out of tripping distance or are securely taped to the floor with wide, strong tape.

In general, make sure there is space for everyone you've invited. Not many people like to be crammed into a space with little area to move around in—especially if they don't already know one another. Some may call it "breathing room".

When designing your floor plan, you want to make sure that you have enough tables and chairs for all your guests to feel comfortable. If your party is very casual, you will want to make sure that you have enough seats for a minimum of 85–90 percent of your guests. Why not 100 percent? This is because not everyone will be sitting at the same time. Not everyone will show up and not everyone will be there at exactly the same time. If your party is more formal, then have space for 105 percent of your guests, because you do not want a single guest at a formal gathering having to stand. It is far better to have more than enough chairs and table space for a formal get-together.

Place chairs and other furniture like couches or benches in an area large enough to hold the majority of your guests. Try to make it feel like a "circle" such that there isn't a lone chair by itself and therefore allowing someone to be excluded from the rest of the group. It is not likely that people will rearrange your furniture layout much, so it is your responsibility, as host, to keep everyone included.

Room Diagram 1

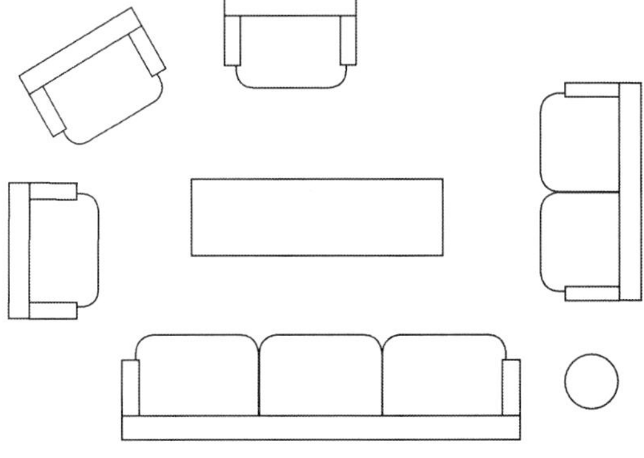

If there is space outside the "circle" for more chairs, it is okay to add chairs in pairs or sets of three or more. If you are working with two chairs, put the front corner of the first chair near the front corner of the second chair close to each other at an angle so the front of the chairs softly face each other. Avoid facing a pair of chairs dead-on or exactly side by side. The soft angle just described, will encourage people to talk to each other without staring at each other. You may want to add a small table between the chairs for cups or plates or snack foods. Keep in mind, you can have more than one "circle", although having everyone close together is ideal.

Try to avoid long buffet tables where all tables are end to end, this keeps the people at each end away from all the other conversations that are occurring. Rather, try to put long buffet tables where the long sides are parallel with people sitting between the tables. This allows multi-table conversation. Round tables are better for groups. I say "try" to avoid this layout, but sometimes it can't be helped. At my Aunt Jane's house this is the only table layout that fits her floor plan-so that's what we do.

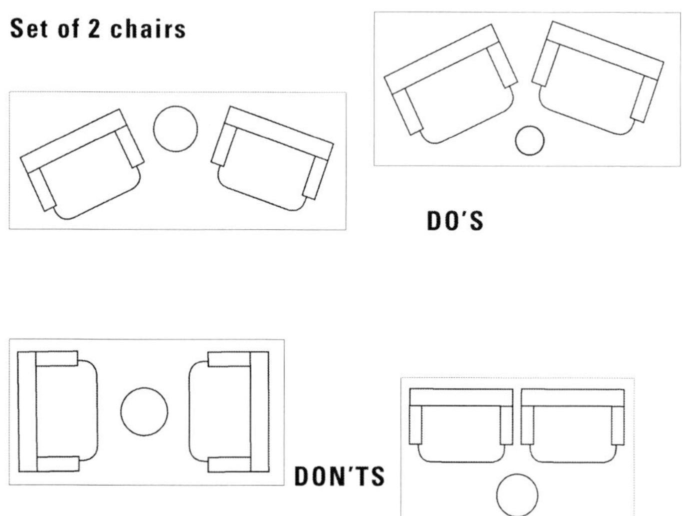

Set of 3 chairs

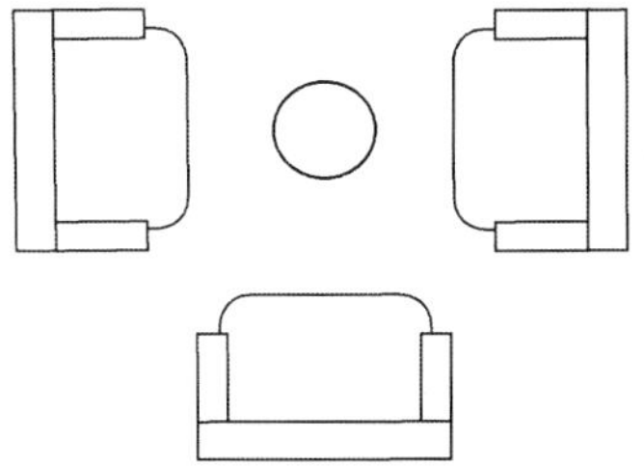

Large Groups Table Diagram

DO'S

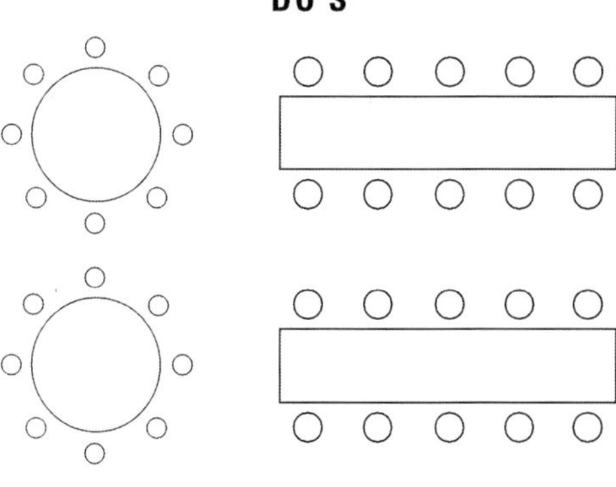

DON'T

People will gather in the space you have created for them, if they feel comfortable in that space. Most people reading this book will be planning for parties in their homes, meaning that the space for your party will most likely be centered in the living room, dining room and/or kitchen (for indoor parties) and will likely be centered in the backyard and patio (for outdoor parties).

Keep your "circles" or party space, and main food area/kitchen and buffet line close together. Doing so will help you avoid:

- Having starving people who can't get to the food
- Having tons of food left over
- Having people gathering in places you don't want them to gather in
- Having people standing the whole time possibly creating traffic flow problems

DESIGN

After you have designed the spatial layout and floor plan be sure to have snack foods out in various places on end tables, near lamps, wherever you think the people will be. Snacks give people something to do, something to talk about, and something to feel (less hungry, more comfortable) and it gives them an excuse to move—either to come over to a certain area or an excuse to leave a certain area. Keep an eye on your snacks, keep them replenished if they run low. Some people will avoid eating food items because they don't want to eat the last of an item. There are some limiting psychological thoughts about finishing off all of someone else's food or the fear of being thought of as "hogging the food". This can keep snack bowls from being emptied completely. Although most hosts would rather guests eat remaining items than have to pack up two cookies, for example. You will want to have some servings of snack foods out for your first guests and keep an extra stash of some kind left over in case you have people stay longer than you expected.

Apply the same smooth and flowing traffic design to your food tables. I recommend a buffet style line for serving food. It is the fastest way to get several people fed in a short amount of time. Not to mention, there is less food wasted because your guests pick and choose what they want to eat rather than having a little bit of everything handed to them, only to be later thrown away. Remember to set your up and plan your buffet line using the water principle so the line flows smoothly and all food is easily accessible.

One final thought for spatial layout is you want to have placed a radio or CD player strategically somewhere in your party space. Strategically means out of the way, not on any usable surface. The source of your music should be heard, not seen.

Design your Music Selection

Music is a great way to create and maintain the mood and atmosphere. Having the right volume is more important than what is actually playing. If you are playing the radio, you can have two stereos in separate locations to spread out the sound and therefore control the volume better. The same goes for those fortunate few with in-house sound systems that can play through speakers in every room. When doing multiple rooms of sound, you can, and should, play the same song in each room. Having different songs overlapping each other is a distraction.

Keep the volume to a minimum. The ideal level is loud enough to be heard on the far side of the room, but soft enough that no one has to raise their voice to talk over the sound. This is definitely something to address at parties where a DJ is present; as he may not realize he is playing the music too loudly for your guests or for the environment you are trying to create. If you are not sure, err on the side of too soft. If you only have one radio, stereo, or CD player, still use it, but only have it loud enough for one room to hear it. For outdoor parties, the same principles apply, have the volume set for your guests to hear it, not the neighborhood—you don't need the cops crashing your party for noise violations.

Choose music that fits the mood you are trying to create. Choose music that is not offensive to the masses. Avoid violent lyrics with cuss words. Rather, choose up-beat music or popular songs that your guests will recognize. When determining what to play, a good indicator of how a song will affect your guests is how it affects you. If you feel happy, or feel like dancing, it's a good choice. If you feel sad, or depressed at what should be a happy event—skip it! Play music that is appropriate and helps create your ideal environment.

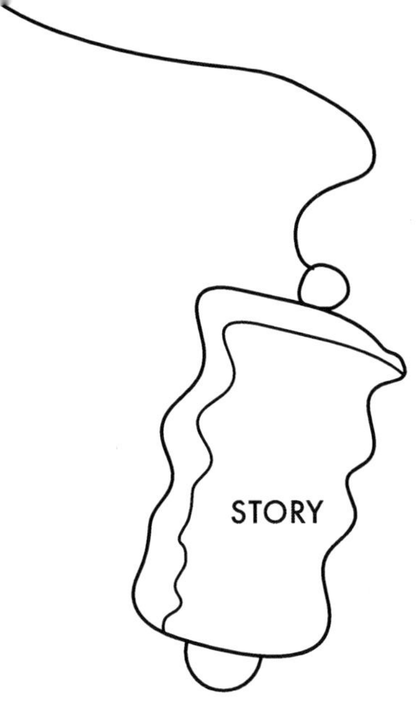

Several of my family members and I went to a funeral of a dear friend. We wanted to be there for a while to offer support to the mother of the woman who had died unexpectedly. We noticed that the room was full of beautiful flowers, was nicely decorated, had chairs, couches and tissues for everyone and the lighting was very complementary. The one thing that didn't seem quite right was the music. The song, playing through the speakers, was appropriate for the solemn occasion but it kept playing over and over. The same song played for hours and hours.

Perhaps it was the favorite song of the woman who died, but for her husband, parents or anyone else who heard it repeated over and over, they are going to subconsciously have it anchored to that occasion, that memory and the feelings they were feeling at the funeral.

So the next time that song is played anywhere, people are going to get very sad and probably flash back to this event–and they won't know why they feel so bad. The funeral coordinator should have suggested a mix of appropriate music as to not prolong the grief for the family of the deceased.

Design your Hosting Boundaries

Determine whether you want to act as *wait staff* for your party or as a *host* for your party.

DESIGN

As *wait staff* you will be getting up to serve every guest's needs and ignoring your own for the duration of the party. For example, you will be getting drinks for everyone, serving food, and clearing plates—everything you'd normally expect a waiter or waitress at a nice restaurant to do, except you'll do all this without receiving tips. This is good if you are having a fancy dinner and you don't want your guests serving themselves or you want to keep people out of your kitchen for whatever reason. There are only a handful of times when this type of service at a party is necessary.

As a *host,* make that, as a really great host, you will do some of the wait staff role but only on the first round. What does that mean? You will not wait on your guests the entire time; rather you'll get them started. Offer your guests a list of what you have for them to drink, then serve the first round, while showing them where it is and telling them to help themselves from now on . . . and then you're off the hook. You may even make a light hearted comment that "this isn't a restaurant; you can help yourself. It's okay." The *host* technique is the recommended approach as it frees you up to do what you want to do, eat, drink, attend to others, and enjoy the party too. Even in host mode you will want to perform some waitstaff duties. You will want to throw away trash when you see it and clear plates and cups when they are left when a guest moves to a different room. These steps will help cut down clean up time later. Check bathroom towels, toilet paper, and snack bowls as well.

Design your Lighting

Lighting, by itself, will greatly influence the feel and emotion of your atmosphere. Dim, soft, lights create a cozy, more intimate feeling between guests. Note that this type of lighting specifically excludes other people in the room, whereas standard lights create a warm, welcome feeling for groups larger than two people. The brightest lights, for example, as used in gymnasiums, hospitals and stadiums to create a more alert and possibly energetic feel. However, they can also create a stark, uninviting and plain feeling, almost like being exposed and somewhat uncomfortable depending on how the bright lights are being used.

The best way to test the effects of lighting are to visit various places that utilize specific lighting schemes and notice how you feel. Compare the lights at your home with those hanging from the ceiling at Wal-Mart or Sam's Club. That will give you a contrast between the standard light and the bright lights. Then visit a nice billiard/pool hall or a fancy, expensive restaurant for dim lighting. Notice at the pool hall and restaurant, that the lights are specifically designed to force the focus between the few people involved and to specifically keep people at other tables out of your "circle".

Now try different lighting options at home. Using the same approximate time as your party, begin by turning on all the lights in the room(s) you will center your party in. How does that make you feel? Do you feel like shutting all the blinds and curtains so you are not on display? Or are you invigorated by having every corner lit up for people to enjoy? Next, turn off half the lights so that the room is still fully illuminated, just not so brightly. How does this change the atmosphere of the room? Perhaps it is more comfortable. Now, try turning on only the lights on one side of the room so that there are darker areas, or try moving a lamp around to different tables in the room. Finally, turn off all but one or two of the lights, or only use candles and see how that affects the room and how it feels. What atmosphere best suits your plan?

Another option with the lights available now is the use of colored light bulbs. Home decor stores sell pastel-colored light bulbs in shades like soft pink or soft blue. You can also go with a drastic change in color by choosing to use red, orange, green or blue light bulbs for a complete change. And then there are black lights which make any light colored or bright colored fabric appear to glow in the dark. You can find these drastically colored bulbs at specialty stores at the mall and sometimes you can find them in the lighting department of stores like Wal-Mart, Target, K-Mart, Kohl's, Dillards, etc.

Lighting an outdoor area can be trickier than an indoor area simply because there are often fewer lighting options available to you. You may already have spot lights in your back yard/patio or a streetlight-type of light in a park. These fall under the "brightest lights" category. Some pavilions or canopies have standard lights and therefore are similar to indoor lighting. Some places don't have any lights at all and are then limited to the small amount of light provided by lanterns, campfires, flashlights, candles, and the moon . . . Hey, you never know.

Outdoor lighting is best executed by supplementing the standard lights with smaller lights. Try to stay away from using the brightest lights as they are hard on the eyes at night.

Design your Ultimate Game Plan

This is where you design your activities within the boundaries of your party. You could call it the time frame, the agenda or the itinerary of your party. Relax, you don't necessarily have to put this in writing, unless you have vendors or people involved in executing your plans, who will need to know what is happening when. The only time when I found putting the ultimate game plan into writing was necessary was for weddings. For parties that are less formal or for those which don't have strict time limits, you will want to mentally create a game plan, but don't have to spell it out on paper.

The ultimate game plan is best being backed into. Starting with the time when your guests arrive and proceeding backward in time until you get to the very beginning of your preparation. That will tell you your ultimate start time so you are not rushed or caught off guard. Next, you will work forward from the point that your guests arrive until the party is over. Then add 30 minutes for clean up. That will give you your ultimate end time so you will know how long you are on the hook for this party. Your prep time doesn't need to include time for grocery shopping unless you are actually shopping on the day of the party. It is not recommended that you wait until the last minute. I suggest the groceries be purchased a least a day ahead of time. If you are buying party trays, then obviously you can't get them too early or they will spoil. Basically, include only pertinent time frames in this game plan.

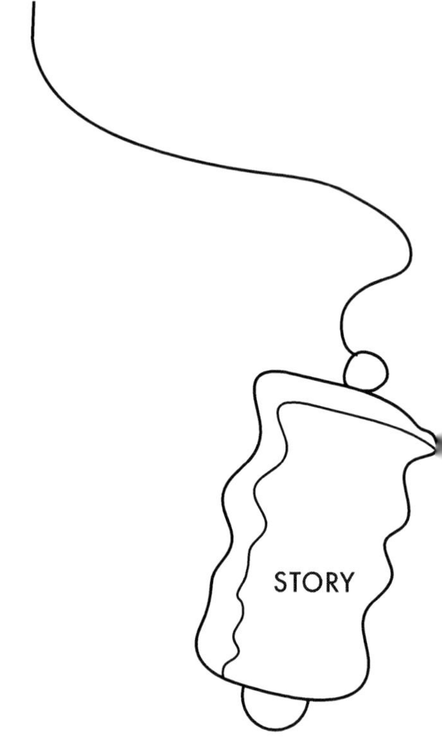

I hosted a formal dinner party for my husband's birthday and set up my mental game plan like this:

__If guests are arriving at 5:30 and I know that I want dinner to be relaxed, and the plan is to leave here to go dancing around 8:00, that gives me 2 ½ hours with people here.

__Since I am serving dinner (Wait staff style) I will need to dress by 5:15 and have the food prepared (with only minor details left undone) by 4:50.

__I already have my menu planned and based on the three courses I am serving; I will need about an hour and 15 minutes to cook and 40 minutes to prepare the ingredients. That puts me at 2:55.

__I will need to decorate so I will do that in the morning, or I can ask a friend to come over the night before and help me hang all the streamers. I can add the helium balloons at about 1:00 so they won't deflate too quickly. (Need to buy balloons and helium tank at Wal-mart one day before.)

__Make list of ingredients and get groceries the day before.

__Great, I have the whole morning to do anything I might have forgotten.

__Now for the party part: if guest arrive at 5:30, they probably won't all arrive at the same time so I will have drinks out and a few snack foods.

__Then I will officially serve dinner at 6:00 and be done by around 7:30.

__I expect that we'll sit around for a bit and talk after dinner.

__A few minutes before 8:00 I'll suggest we get going to the dance place. (As no reservations are necessary.)

__I'll have directions and the address on pieces of paper for everyone, ready to hand out and then we'll go dancing.

__Since the band plays until midnight, and I don't think my guests will come back here after dancing, it will probably end there, at or before midnight.

__I will have done as much clean up of dishes while cooking as possible so all I'll need to do when we get home is throw a few dishes in the dishwasher and start the machine washing dishes—30 minutes, no problem.

Your ultimate game plan will give you an accurate time frame that you will be involved in the party. Your plan may be even less detailed than mine.

After going through this process, you will want to write down a check list of things to do and/or remember. You can't pick up a party tray if you have forgotten to order it in time. Keep the list on one piece of paper and in one place. Always write things down when you think about them or when your mind is relaxed. This will help to avoid last minute rushing.

Design your Vision

Visualization can be one of the most beneficial steps you can take when preparing for a party. What do I mean *visualize?* I mean picture it. You have done some preliminary visualization work when you designed your ultimate game plan. This step gets into more detail. Keep in mind that your designing work is done by this point in the planning process. So, the hard part is over.

Imagine in your mind your party is in full swing. As you look around your event space, picture in your mind who is sitting where, which people are on the couch talking, who is hovering around the food? What kind of lighting are you using? What is the mood? Are there children running around? Will the kids be playing around the adults or will you have a separate area to keep them occupied? What music is playing in the background? How is your food laid out?

You don't have to imagine every minute, especially because it will likely not occur as you imagine it. Do, however, mentally go through the main parts. Imagine the food and the activities you've planned. When will things happen? How long is it going to last? Now imagine which guests will stay the longest. Who will be the last ones to leave? Of course, unless you are psychic, you won't know these for certain, but you will feel and be more prepared.

This is an important step in the planning process, even though it is a quick and easy one. It is often skipped and shouldn't be. Performing this visualization technique will give you a better understanding of everything and help remind you of things you may have forgotten. Believe it or not, doing this visualization will greatly improve your odds of actually experiencing the images you mentally create.

Visualize most of, if not the entire, party. When you visualize, add these few details:

- Every person you envision at your party is smiling and having a great time.
- Every person you envision is engaged in an activity such as a conversation, playing a game, eating, drinking, laughing, or any combination of these.
- You are relaxed, calm, smiling, laughing, having a fantastic time, and are involved in the party too.

DESIGN

your Atmosphere / Mood - your ultimate feeling

your Invitations - evoke emotion and reaction

your Decorations - create a fabulous environment

your Spatial Layout / Floor plan - traffic flow and furniture

your Music Selection - volume over selection

your Hosting Boundaries - wait staff or host

your Lighting - bright or dim, how 'bout color

your Ultimate Game Plan - the timing, agenda or itinerary

your Vision - see what your party will look like before it starts

Conclusion/Final Thought: If you have designed the details to support your expectations as well as support your guests, it will indirectly have a positive influence on everyone involved. All will enjoy themselves and no one will know why.

Chapter Three

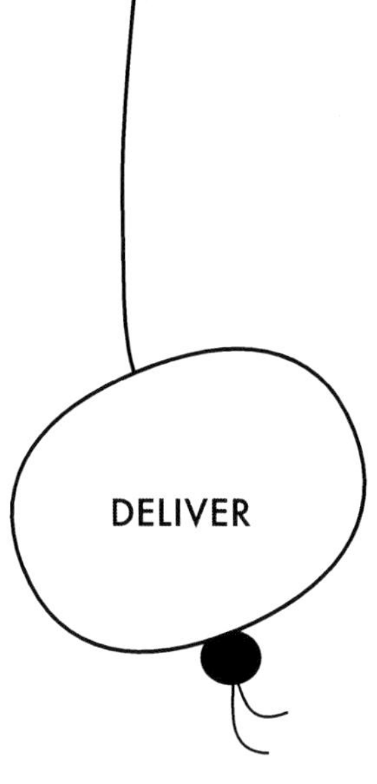

Delivery is the time to set your plan in motion. It is here that you make your dreams a reality. It is through action that we reap our rewards and our greatness is recognized. Experience your vision! Go for it! Be the greatest host ever. Have the party people will talk about for years to come.

Here's what to DO:

Deliver your Before-the-Party Actions

Double check directions you are going to give out. Find out if there will be new road construction that might affect your directions between now and the party.

Invites - send them at least 2 weeks ahead of time and then call if you need to have a head count. Include a road map if the directions are complicated.

Make one checklist of everything you want/need to remember.

Order food, buy food, or pick up food.

Arrange for a babysitter, if necessary.

Clean up before party - this is a MUST DO. Do the dishes, clear off 90% of your counter space, vacuum, dust, clean and change the towels in the bathroom, wash your dirty laundry and then put away clean laundry, make your bed and take out the trash. If you don't like to clean, hire someone else to do it. Trust me on this. Keep in mind that the condition of your house is when guests arrive, is the way it will be when they leave, if not worse. Set the standard very high, it will make the clean up *after* the party easier. People will think that if *you* trash your house, they can too. If your house looks pristine like a magazine cover, your guests will be very careful to keep it that way. It's an unwritten rule, go ahead, test it.

Arrange, or rearrange, your furniture using the water principle and the no 90 degree angle rules.

Make your location easy to find. Turn on porch lights to make addresses easier to find, put out balloons or signs or use obvious landmarks to help navigate people to where you are.

Deliver your This-Point-Forward, Freedom from Stress Actions

Just before your party begins, you have one final step to make that will make or break this party experience for you as the host. This is vital to your success. You need to take in a deep breath and say out loud, with an attitude and feeling of certainty, the following declarations:

> "Whatever is going to happen, will happen, and at this moment, I choose not to change it.
>
> I have fun without stress.
>
> I am free from all anxiety from this point forward.

Unexpected circumstances will be handled with ease, grace and in a calm state of mind.

Unexpected events will make memories for me and my guests to enjoy.

I release all negative thoughts and negative energy about what may go wrong and I focus only on what I want and what I enjoy.

I know that I can handle anything and everything that comes up and I will make the best of every situation.

With every moment, I find a reason to smile, laugh out loud and celebrate even more fully.

This is MY event and I choose here and now to enjoy every minute of it!"

Now, take another deep breath and feel how great it is when you are in control of your attitude and emotions right now. Take a moment for yourself. You have worked diligently to plan and prepare for this event, and you already deserve a pat on the back for your accomplishments.

Get ready, set, go! Let's get this party started!

Deliver your As-Each-Guest-Arrives Actions

Give a quick tour of your location whether it is your home, a banquet hall or any other place. Show guests all the rooms if possible. You must point out where the bathrooms are.

Giving a tour achieves several goals.

a) Humans are naturally curious animals; a tour alleviates that curiosity, and they are less likely to snoop around after the tour.

b) People are more likely to feel comfortable and avoid embarrassment when they don't have to ask where the restrooms are located.

c) It frees you from giving how-to and where-is-it directions the entire time.

d) It is an unconscious gesture that softly says, "You are welcome here. What's mine is yours, and I want you to know everything you need to know. I am laying everything out on the table for you to see and I have nothing to hide."

DELIVER

A tour, given during a person's first visit to your location, is a fantastic and important first move on your part, and it will do wonders for your party.

Tell people what you expect and what they should expect. Doing this, will increase the chances of having what you expect actually happen. You can casually mention about what time the games will start, or when the main food will be served, or that you'd like people to remain in these specific rooms, or that you need to find someone to volunteer to grill hamburgers. This step is amazing for creating action on the part of your guests without you as the host having to play "party police". This step creates anticipation and excitement, opens the line of communication, and releases anxiety and stress.

Deliver your During-the-Party Actions

You will want to occasionally:

Check to make sure there are 2 extra rolls of toilet paper in plain sight in each bathroom. Don't make your guests hunt, because they probably won't. Yikes!

Change the hand towels in bathroom if you have lots of guests. Yes, I know you just did that before the party, but you may need to do it again during the party. The more people you have, the wetter and dirtier they will be. Switch them out half way through the party to make sure your guests have dry towels to use. It is a little step that will make you stand out as an incredible host.

Check all the trash containers. If they are full, empty them. This includes the bathroom.

Wash your hands and then refill snack foods bowls and replenish the supply of napkins, cups, plates, etc.

Ask for help with things you need done. This will keep guests involved and most everyone will be happy to help you out anyway, so you should take advantage of the opportunity.

Clean up during the party - pick up trash and empty cups, stack the dirty (washable) dishes by the sink or put them directly into the dishwasher. It is okay to rinse dishes, but don't wash dishes during the party—your guests may feel awkward as if they should be cleaning too.

Deliver your Generally-Speaking Actions

Always consider the needs of your guests, and do your absolute best to anticipate them and prepare for them.

If people are clearing their trash or dishes, let them. Don't put off someone cleaning up after themselves, it's less for you to do. Besides, they may have another reason for getting up, perhaps it's an excuse to refill a drink or discreetly use the restroom. Maybe they are just being nice, so let them. It's okay to tell them "You don't have to do that.", but don't make a big deal about it. If they insist, simply say thank you.

If you have a spouse or significant other, have them either be 95% present or 99% gone. It will be a distraction to your guests to have your immediate family coming and going, in and out of your party.

Be sure to attend your own party, it defeats the purpose if you are not enjoying yourself or are uninvolved. Guests always notice the host's actions.

Leave personal problems, attitudes and prejudices outside of your party. If you are happy, the guests will be too. You cannot necessarily control what happens at your gathering. You can however, control your reactions to these things and therefore control the reactions of your guests in the same way.

DESIGN

Deliver your After-the-Party Actions

Clean up after the party, if all the prior steps are done then clean-up will be a cinch. It shouldn't take more than 30 minutes to complete.

Put all open food in sealed containers and put in refrigerator if necessary.

Remove or take down decorations.

Double check that all candles are blown out.

Start the dishwasher and take out the trash.

Go to bed and get a good night's sleep. You can call your best friend and re-experience the whole thing all over again, detail by detail, tomorrow.

Make mental notes of anything you will do differently or exactly the same next time. Then write me a letter sharing all the details, what you did, what you learned, how you feel afterwards, what specific ideas you used from this book that helped you host an incredible party.

What NOT to Do

I was invited to a stay-over-night new year's eve party. Guests were to bring a dish to share, a gift for a gift exchange and a change of clothes with sleeping bags. Put bluntly, this was more of a horror story from my perspective. When I arrived, her house was very cluttered and dirty. The host had invited about 60 people, although the furniture was limited to a 2-person love seat in the living room and four kitchen chairs. I put my dish-to-share in the kitchen and my coat and gift in one of the bedrooms with the other coats and gifts. I had barely set my things down when the host asked me and my boyfriend at the time, to go back out in the cold and to pick up several bags of ice. We were happy to help, although the host seemed completely oblivious to the fact that we had just driven over two hours in bad weather to get there in the first place and she could have easily called our cell phones ten minutes earlier to ask for ice. Anyway, we went to get ice because we are nice people.

When he and I returned, more people had arrived. The party which had started out slow soon picked up. We carried in several bags of ice but discovered there was no where to put them. I went to the kitchen sink as a place to put the ice while the host ventured into the garage to see if she could find a cooler "or something". The sink was FULL of dirty dishes! These were not the dishes used to prepare for the party; they were dirty dishes from several days ago. I could tell by the dried, stuck-on food that they'd been there a while.

In my attempt to quickly find an alternative place to store the bags of ice, and feeling my hands going numb from the cold, I noticed the dish-drying rack next to the sink. But it too was full of dishes. I thought to myself, "I hope those are clean dishes," just before I noticed the drying rack had some serious cobwebs on it! I should have known with that discovery that it wouldn't be the last unpleasant surprise.

There wasn't much mingling and meeting of new people going on since the host made no attempt to introduce guests to each other. The cliques of friends formed as they usually do, in different areas of the house. Most of the guests were drinking alcohol as a way to celebrate the New Year and by midnight had gotten pretty sloshed. Thinking the "big moment" had now passed; people began to leave the party just after the twelve o'clock hour. In a disorganized fashion the host put the word out that she now wanted to do the gift exchange. She started arbitrarily handing out gifts, but soon realized that about half of them were missing. They had been stolen! She had had no plan to keep an eye on them, so I can't say I was completely surprised.

Since I personally choose not to drink alcohol, I didn't feel much like part of the party. Getting drunk seemed the main source of entertainment at this event. So, either out of boredom or the desire to leave the place in better condition then the way I found it (a trait I picked up from my mother), I began to clean the kitchen. Believe me, there was plenty to do. The host came in after a while and told me, "You don't have to do the dishes". I knew that, but what else was I going to do?

I cleaned literally for several hours. I washed dishes, wiped down cabinets, picked up bits of trash from the floor, I scrubbed her stove top, removed splattered grease from the side of her refrigerator, rewashed the dishes in the dish drying rack (at least I hope re-washed is the right word), cleared off and cleaned the countertops, wiped down the sticky handles of the refrigerator, and emptied the trash can which was of course over-flowing with trash. It turns out she had a very nice kitchen—when you could see the surfaces.

I went to use the restroom and found it was also neglected like a truck stop bathroom on a bad day. There was barely enough toilet paper to cover the cardboard tube. There was no soap, the trash was over flowing onto the floor and the hand towels soaked enough to drip. I'll admit that I snooped around long enough to find a roll of toilet paper. After all, I had waited in line for this opportunity to use the restroom.

The party wound down about 3:00 A.M. and those who had prearranged to stay overnight prepared for sleep by unrolling their sleeping bags and blankets and changing into pajamas. Others, who were too intoxicated to drive, tried to squish on the 2-person love seat or had already passed out on the floor. There were bodies everywhere. I figured tomorrow had to be better than this and went to sleep.

People woke up intermittently and waited for the host to give some hint as to what was for breakfast. She poked around in the refrigerator, obviously unsure what to prepare and eventually pulled out a few ingredients. She started making an unidentified egg dish that had to be baked in the oven for over 45 minutes. People began picking at and eating food from the evening before that had been sitting out, uncovered, all night. By the time she actually put it in the oven, everyone was awake and starving. The host sat down acted as if she was done making breakfast. I couldn't believe she was only making ONE small thing for breakfast to feed all of the people there. The serving of this egg dish we each got was smaller than the palm of my hand and did not fill anyone up.

Someone I did not know, out of sheer desperation, raided the refrigerator and found a package of bacon. Halleluiah, there is more to eat! The host was surprised it was in there and began cooking it. Yikes! How old is that bacon?

I watched in disbelief as she grabbed a clean fork, probably one I washed just hours before, from the silverware drawer and moved the bacon around in the frying pan before she threw it in the sink as a dirty dish. She then pulled another clean one out of the drawer and did the same thing. This happened about three times. My jaw dropped farther and farther after each fork landed with a "tink" sound in the sink. I could not believe it! After I washed dishes all night and scrubbed her kitchen down thoroughly, how could she have the audacity to be so wasteful in front of me? Keep in mind, I could understand the need for lots of extra dirty dishes, if she had been preparing several different food items, but she WASN'T! This was one package of bacon in one pan. How ungrateful!!!

I never went to another party at her house again. I was hungry, felt unappreciated as a volunteer and ignored as a guest. I don't have to work half as hard when I host parties by myself.

That party was the worst one I have ever been to. Please use it as an example of what NOT to do at your parties.

~

Now that you have read most of this book, never go to a party and correct the host or point out when they aren't following the suggestions in this book. That would be rude and could offend your host. You can, however, make friendly suggestions to the host and offer to make the change for them or offer to help them out, but allow them to decline your offer. Don't force your way on the host at someone else's party. After the party is over, you can do two things:

1) Give them a copy of this book as a gift and thank them for a wonderful time at *their* party, and

2) Learn from their way of hosting what you will do differently at your next party. What I learned from the Horror Story you just read allowed me to host my first over-night Mardi Gras party where I planned and anticipated for every need of my guests.

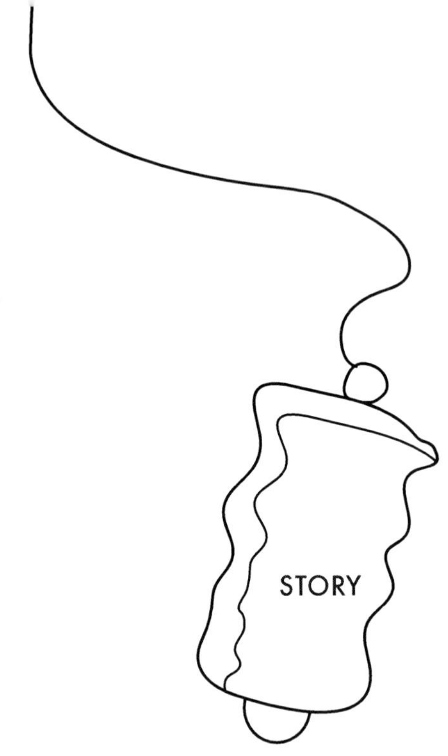

I was part of a close group of friends that all enjoyed East Coast Swing dancing when I lived in Michigan. While I was involved with this great group of people, my boyfriend and I decided we would host an overnight Mardi Gras party for this group of people. We didn't hold anything back on this one and therefore had to start planning and preparing early. About a month or two before the party, we started making plans for the "party of all parties". Without telling our friends what we were up to, we asked them to borrow any photos of this group. Since we went to many, many events and dances together, lots of photos came in. He and I spent several hours over several weekends scanning all the photos onto a computer.

Since the party was going to be held in all rooms of his house including the basement, we made some improvements. We moved all the items stored in the basement to one corner and stained his entire basement floor to cover up scuff marks or cracks. We then bought cloth material to hang from the ceiling to cover up all the corner stuff so it would be out of sight. Once the floor was ready, we set up the ping pong table and a dance floor area with seating for both sides. The ping pong area of the basement had bright lights to play by and had cloth hanging down as temporary "walls" to keep the ping pong balls from flying uncontrollably onto the dance floor. For the dance floor we purchased a small mirror ball, several cheap colored directional lights and spread glitter on the floor. We programmed the CD player in the basement to play hours of the group's favorite dance songs so that no one would have to change CDs or have the music stop in the middle of the party.

Since my boyfriend was in the audio-visual business, his house already had the whole-house sound system so the music could be played in all the rooms simultaneously. He also wired the television in the family room to his computer in his home office so the photos we scanned would loop continuously as a slide show during the party. This allowed us to honor and celebrate each of our guests and our friendship with them. Since it was still winter and it would be dark before seven o'clock in the evening, we bought lights to string up on decorative landscape posts to illuminate the front walkway.

We sent out our invitations early with all the instructions and details so our guests would have enough time to prepare to fully participate in the events of the evening. The invites explained the dress code, the gag gift exchange instructions, what to bring for the overnight (pajamas, sleeping bags, etc) and directions on how to find his house easily in the dark.

We moved furniture around in the bedrooms to make room for extra floor space and sleeping bags. We also made sure there were extra blankets, pillows, and bath towels on hand (for the morning after). We put fresh, clean sheets on all the beds for the first takers. We planned to provide all the food so we set out everything for the evening.

One of the other couples showed up early to help us decorate the rest of the house. Things started out normal although it got a little crazy when the personalities mixed with the helium tank both before and during the party. On the first floor we decorated the living room, dining room, family room and kitchen with unmatched color streamers and helium filled balloons.

The party theme was multi-part. It was an overnight, Mardi Gras Party with a costume contest and gag gift exchange. First, all the guests were required to dress for the theme but with a twist. The guests were all participating in a "Worst Dressed Contest". I shopped at a thrift store and found a dress with a black velvet long-sleeved top part and a floor length skirt part that was made from literally 1 ½ inch thick quilt material with huge, bright yellow and orange flowers on it. It looked like someone had decided to take the comforter off their bed and make a dress out of it. This was a classic design I have never see again. My boyfriend found a brown and pink striped suit to wear. Our guests all arrived in costume and played full out. There were strings of different colored, different sized Mardi Gras beads everywhere and on everyone.

A few of the women in the group decided to hand-make each person a mask to reflect some aspect of their personality. Since I love tigers, they made mine to look like a tiger. The masks were a wonderful and unexpected addition to the party theme that really livened up the event. As each guest arrived, they put their gag gift in a laundry basket that was stored in a closet to keep it out of the way. Once everyone was there, and the sleeping bags were in the bedrooms and the guests had their food and beverage in hand, we started their surprise. We showed them the picture slide show. They were so surprised and excited since they had no idea. The slide show lasted a little over an hour after all the contributions they gave us, but it brought back many great memories and was a great way to open the party. There was lots of laughter and comments throughout the show. The slide show alone went over so well, it would have made a great party theme by itself. After that, we did the tour so our guest would know what was where and then the party took off. There was lots of eating, drinking, laughing, picture posing, playing, and fun. There wasn't as much dancing as I had expected, but it was a nice touch and there was so much going on.

We soon handed out ballots to vote for the King and Queen of the Worst Dressed Mardi Gras party. Since the other outfits were even more hideous than mine, it was a hard decision. The winners got plastic crowns to proudly wear.

When things started slowing down, and the impromptu ping pong tournament was over, we got out the gag gifts and did our exchange. Well into the night, we settled in and went to sleep. As the host, I stayed up a little bit longer to put the open food up that would have spoiled overnight. The next morning, we got up and made a massive breakfast. We had a dozen or so scrambled eggs, over-easy and sunny-side-up eggs upon request, bacon, sausage, several kinds of cereal, milk, orange juice, apple juice, coffee, white and wheat toast, English muffins and a huge selection of fruits and things to eat. Some people showered before breakfast to allow for the water heater to prepare for those showering after breakfast. After breakfast, there was more ping pong and fun. That afternoon, people packed up their things and started heading off. This was a blast.

All the advanced planning and preparation paid off. No detail got missed or overlooked. Keep in mind though, I couldn't have pulled off this unbelievable party if I hadn't already experienced and learned so much from the one prior to it.

DELIVER

your Before the Party actions

your As Each Guest Arrives actions

your During the Party actions

your Generally Speaking actions

your After the Party actions

Conclusion/Final Thought: If you will deliver to your guests what you have decided and designed, it will be a success and you will be a fantastic host. You will be prepared, enjoy yourself and you will avoid being burdened and stressed out. Just relish the fond memories of good times had by all.

Chapter Four

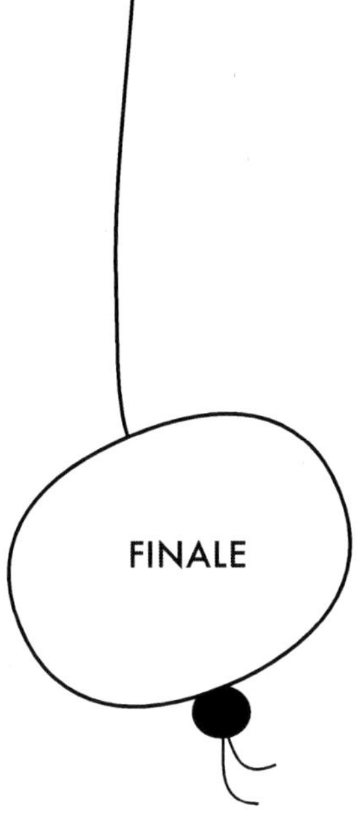

Remember that "Moment of Truth" I mentioned on the first few pages? Let's talk about that. You can easily tell that your party was successful. Just answer to yourself these few questions:

What was great about that?

What did I enjoy most?

What was the funniest thing that happened?

What story about this party is going to be told over and over?

What did people say about this party? That they had fun? . . . Enjoyed themselves? . . . Hated to leave? . . . Can't wait for the next one?

Who did I invite that showed up?

Who at my party seemed relaxed, talked to others, laughed out loud or smiled?

If you are able to answer any of these questions, it was great party. Good job!

Note from the Author

I want to thank you for reading this book. It was my pleasure to share my knowledge, skills, and passion with you. I am honored to have my thoughts and ideas being used nationwide and hopefully world wide.

I welcome any party planning questions you may have. As well as any wedding stories you have either as the host or as a guest. Currently, I am working toward writing magazine columns through which I can discuss ideas in more specific detail and have other books in progress. Please mail your ideas, stories, and questions to the address listed below. As mentioned earlier, I also welcome feedback about this book in particular: how well your first party after reading this book went over, what you learned, what specific ideas were used from this book that helped to host an incredible party or any other thoughts you'd like to share.

Mail to:

Angel Elder
8801 N. Western Avenue
Oklahoma City, OK 73114

or visit the website at:

www.tamingpartychaos.com

With love and gratitude,

Angel Elder

About The Author

As a lover of parties and host of hundreds herself, Angel B. L. Elder spent her adolescent years experiencing parties the way others hosted them and has spent her adult years improving the process, having learned from her predecessors, and hosting enhanced parties the way she describes in this book.

Born into a very large family that celebrates every special occasion, she learned masterful ways to host social engagements with large groups in small spaces on limited budgets. As soon as Angel was old enough, she was carrying on the family celebration traditions while testing new and outrageous ideas, creating novel experiences for her guests and always trying to raise the standard of excellence in the field of event planning or social gatherings. Excited to share her skills with the world, Angel wants to eradicate poor planning that leads to negative social experiences.

> **"Make a point to laugh out loud and find something to celebrate every day."–Angel Elder**

In the field of party planning, Angel hopes that this book will inspire and encourage the fearful, help direct the mildly experienced and aid in creativity and continued enhancement for the professionals.

TATE PUBLISHING & *Enterprises*

Tate Publishing is committed to excellence in the publishing industry. Our staff of highly trained professionals, including editors, graphic designers, and marketing personnel, work together to produce the very finest books available. The company reflects the philosophy established by the founders, based on Psalms 68:11,

"THE LORD GAVE THE WORD AND GREAT WAS THE COMPANY OF THOSE WHO PUBLISHED IT."

If you would like further information, please call
1.888.361.9473
or visit our website
www.tatepublishing.com

TATE PUBLISHING & *Enterprises*, LLC
127 E. Trade Center Terrace
Mustang, Oklahoma 73064 USA